One is the Body

One is the Body

Songs of unity and diversity

John L. Bell

WILD GOOSE PUBLICATIONS

First published 2002

ISBN 1 901557 35 9

Copyright © 2002 Wild Goose Resource Group

Published by Wild Goose Publications
Fourth Floor, Savoy House, 140 Sauchiehall Street, Glasgow G2 3DH, UK
www.ionabooks.com

Wild Goose Publications is the publishing division of the Iona Community.
Scottish Charity No. SC003794.
Limited Company Reg.No. SC0096243.

Front cover: Graham Maule © 2002 Wild Goose Resource Group

The Wild Goose Resource Group (John L. Bell & Graham Maule) and the members of
the Wild Goose Worship Group have asserted their rights
under the Copyright, Designs & Patents Act, 1988, to be identified
as the authors of this work.

Distributed in Australia by Willow Connection Pty Ltd,
Unit 4A, 3-9 Kenneth Road, Manly Vale NSW 2093, Australia,
and in New Zealand by Pleroma Christian Supplies, Higginson Street,
Otane 4170, Central Hawkes Bay, New Zealand.

Permission to reproduce any part of this work in Australia or New Zealand should be
sought from Willow Connection.

A catalogue record for this book is available from the British Library.

Printed by Bell & Bain, Thornliebank, Glasgow, UK

Contents

The Word of God

Commitment to God

Introduction

With a very few exceptions, these are *not* new songs.

We don't publish new songs. We write, compose, gather and edit material for specific contexts, and usually use it in Glasgow. Then, if the songs have proved their worth and undergone more fine-tuning they may be offered to a wider constituency. But our aim has never been to write a song of the church or to come up with a best-seller.

The worship of God is too important to be dominated by the latest productions of 'gifted writers'. Public worship is not the place to exhibit private piety or to turn a corporate act into a highly individualistic ritual, even if the tunes are nice.

So, we are indebted to a whole range of people in our Worship Group, at monthly events in Glasgow, at *BIG SINGS* throughout Britain and in small congregational gatherings who used these materials and offered their criticism in order that the hymns and songs should be worthier offerings to God and more accessible to worshippers.

In this, as in our other collections, we have tried to be eclectic in the best sense.

The song of the Church has never been narrowly nationalist, so we have included, often in translation, songs which have come to us from other continents.

The song of the Church has never been highly subjective, so we have been keen to incorporate texts from the Psalms and from scripture which objectively witness to God's will and sometimes probe the more troubled parts of our nature.

The song of the Church has never been homogeneous, so we have included a wide range of styles of text, tune and subject-matter, as well as drawing on our own bank of material from the last sixteen years of working in the areas of music and liturgy.

Only two of these songs have been published in one of our previous books, but twelve have already appeared in octavo anthem form, and over half have been recorded, details of which are appended to the relevant songs.

We hope and pray that the material in this collection may enable those who use it not so much to enjoy the songs as to enjoy God – which is the chief purpose of worship.

John Bell & Graham Maule
for THE WILD GOOSE WORSHIP GROUP
Sept 2001

Gathering for worship

Worship does not happen in a vacuum. It happens, by command and expectation of the living God, within a community of people who gather together specifically to praise their Maker.

There are, of course, moments of private devotion. There are times of deep personal intimacy with God. But the Church does not exist to hallow these. The Church exists to bear witness to God's interest in the community as the prime forum in which God's truth and purposes are revealed, celebrated and responded to in discipleship.

The Church must therefore consciously gather. It is insufficient for unconnected strangers to wander in, sit in isolation and disappear without discerning why they worship or experiencing a sense of welcome and belonging.

In this first section, there are a number of songs which may help to gather people together, rehearse their reason for worshipping and prepare them to engage with their Maker.

Come and let us worship God

Tune: 'COME AND LET US WORSHIP', Cranmer Mugisha.

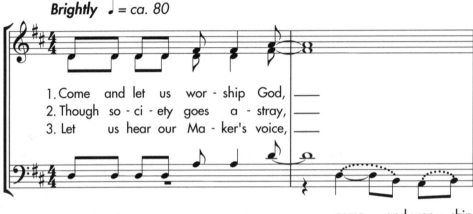

1. Come and let us wor - ship God, ____ come ____ and wor - ship
2. Though so - ci - ety goes a - stray, ____ goes _____ a -
3. Let us hear our Ma - ker's voice, ____ hear ____ our Ma - ker's

turn to serve the li - ving Lord, ____ God, serve ____ the li - ving
keen to find an eas - ier way; ____ stray, find ____ an eas - ier
and let Christ in - form each choice. ____ voice, Christ ____ in - form each

WE, THE CREA - TURES OF YOUR WORD,

COME TO MAKE OUR HOME IN YOU,

KNOW - ING THAT YOUR WORD IS TRUE.

1. Come and let us worship God,
    turn to serve the living Lord,
    move from where we are misled,
    do as ancient prophets said.

    OH, OUR EVER LOVING GOD,
    WE, THE CREATURES OF YOUR WORD,
    COME TO MAKE OUR HOME IN YOU,
    KNOWING THAT YOUR WORD IS TRUE.

2. Though society goes astray,
    keen to find an easier way;
    let our eyes be on God's care,
    evident and everywhere.

3. Let us hear our Maker's voice
    and let Christ inform each choice.
    Sister women, brother men,
    let us turn to God again.

This gathering song is best deployed when a cantor or choir sing each verse and it is immediately repeated by the congregation. It should be both rhythmic and relaxed.

Single copies are available for choirs from the GIA catalogue, G –5160, and the song is featured on the album TAKE THIS MOMENT.

Lord, who may enter your house?

Tune: 'SOJOURNER', John L. Bell.

last time to Final Antiphon
D.C.

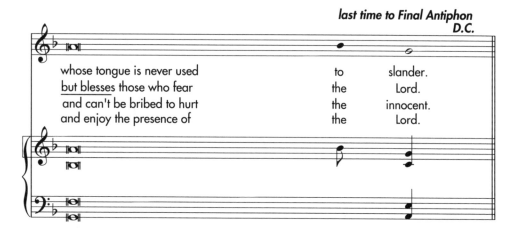

whose tongue is never used   to   slander.
but blesses those who fear   the   Lord.
and can't be bribed to hurt   the   innocent.
and enjoy the presence of   the   Lord.

Final Antiphon: ALL

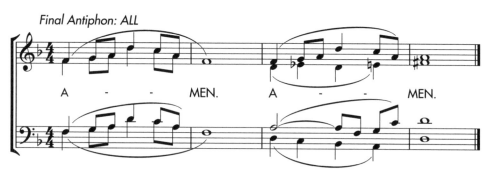

A - - MEN.   A - - MEN.

Antiphon: LORD, WHO MAY ENTER YOUR HOUSE?
        WHO MAY REMAIN IN YOUR PRESENCE?

1.   Whoever leads a blameless life,
        and does what is right;
        who speaks the truth from the heart,
        whose tongue is never used to slander.

2.   Whoever does no wrong to friends,
        nor spreads false rumours about neighbours;
        who does not praise those God condemns,
        but blesses those who fear the Lord.

(continued)

3. Whoever keeps each solemn promise
    no matter what the cost;
    who lends without demanding interest,
    and can't be bribed to hurt the innocent.

4. Those who behave in this way
    will always remain unshaken.
    They may enter God's house
    and enjoy the presence of the Lord.

Final antiphon: AMEN. AMEN.

Psalm 15 is a dialogue between the worshipper who asks a question and God who provides, by way of an answer, a list of attributes which describe the characteristics of committed disciples.

In this setting, the question is posed by the congregation and the answer is offered by the cantor. As with other responsorial psalms, the choir or cantor should sing the antiphon for the first time. It is then repeated by all and sung by all after each verse.

There is no need to keep strict tempo in the verses; the speed is dictated entirely by the cantor's interpretation of the text.

Single copies are available for choirs from the GIA catalogue, G–4669, and the psalm is featured on the album PSALMS OF DAVID AND SONGS OF MARY.

Praise God for this holy ground

Tune: 'HEYMONYSTRAAT', John L. Bell.

1. Praise God for this holy ground,
   place and people, sight and sound.
   Hallelujah! Hallelujah! Hallelujah!
   God's goodness is eternal.

2. Praise God in whose word we find
   food for body, soul and mind.
   Hallelujah! Hallelujah! Hallelujah!
   God's goodness is eternal.

3. Praise God who through Christ makes known
   all are loved and called God's own.
   Hallelujah! Hallelujah! Hallelujah!
   God's goodness is eternal.

4. Praise God's Spirit who befriends,
   raises, humbles, breaks and mends.
   Hallelujah! Hallelujah! Hallelujah!
   God's goodness is eternal.

5. Though praise ends, praise is begun
   where God's will is gladly done.
   Hallelujah! Hallelujah! Hallelujah!
   God's goodness is eternal.

Suitable for use at either beginning or end of worship, this song offers gratitude for the physical space and identifiable people on which and among whom worship takes place.

The text is intended for unison singing with organ accompaniment.

Bless, O my soul, the Lord your God

Tune: 'COLESHILL', 1706 (anonymous).

Paraphrase (of Psalm 103) by John L. Bell, copyright © 1998 WGRG, Iona Community, Glasgow, Scotland.

1. Bless, O my soul, bless God the Lord,
   the one from whom you came;
   let all within me be stirred up
   to bless God's holy name.

2. Bless, O my soul, the Lord your God
   and never once forget
   the many gracious benefits
   God gave and gives you yet.

3. Pardon for all the wrong you've done,
   healing from every ill,
   rescue from ruin and from death –
   these spring from God's good will.

4. God's love and mercy crown your life;
   God meets your deep desires;
   the Lord who makes the eagles soar,
   your new-found life inspires.

5. Bless God, you mighty angel throngs,
   fulfilling heaven's command;
   bless God, all you attendant hosts
   who serve at God's right hand.

6. O bless the Lord, in heaven and earth,
   you creatures of God's word;
   and you, my soul, stir up yourself
   to bless and worship God.

For most of its history, metrical psalm-singing has been the standard diet of the Presbyterian churches in the British Isles. Hymns were relatively uncommon until the 20th century. This style of singing the psalms was also the predominant Anglican use until chant was popularised in the mid-19th century.

The tune 'Coleshill' dates from 1703 and has long been associated with Psalm 103 which sees the offering of the individual's worship in harmony with that of history, creation, heaven and earth.

A choral arrangement of this psalm is found in the GIA catalogue, G4673, and the psalm is featured on the album PSALMS OF DAVID AND SONGS OF MARY.

Blest be God

Tune: 'SENA' Punjabi traditional, Pakistan.

Joyfully ♩ = 104

Refrain

Cantor

Blest be God, praised for e-ver and wor-shipped; blest be God,

praised for e-ver and e-ver. BLEST BE GOD, PRAISED FOR E-VER AND

WOR - SHIPPED; BLEST BE GOD, PRAISED FOR E-VER.

Cantor

1. Blest be God, praised by all times and na - tions.____

ALL

BLEST BE GOD, PRAISED BY ALL TIMES AND NA - TIONS.____

Cantor

Chant the name Yah-weh for e-ver,____ ha-lle-lu-jah!

Original words source unknown, translated by Samuel Paul, versified by James Michin (slightly amended).
Translation copyright © Asian Institute of Liturgy & Music, PO Box 10533, Quezon City 1112, Philippines.

CHANT THE NAME YAH - WEH FOR E - VER, AND WOR - SHIP;

Dal 𝄋

BLEST BE GOD, PRAISED FOR E - VER AND E - VER.

Antiphon:
Cantor: Blest be God, praised for ever and worshipped,
blest be God praised for ever and ever.
ALL: BLEST BE GOD, PRAISED FOR EVER AND WORSHIPPED
BLEST BE GOD, PRAISED FOR EVER.

1. *Cantor:* Blest be God, praised by all times and nations.
ALL: BLEST BE GOD, PRAISED BY ALL TIMES AND NATIONS.
Cantor: Chant the name Yahweh for ever, hallelujah!
ALL: CHANT THE NAME YAHWEH FOR EVER, AND WORSHIP;
BLEST BE GOD, PRAISED FOR EVER AND EVER.

2. *Cantor:* Blest be God, known by each congregation.
ALL: (Repeat)
Cantor: Sing divine praises for ever, hallelujah!
ALL: SING DIVINE PRAISES FOR EVER, AND WORSHIP;
BLEST BE GOD, PRAISED FOR EVER AND EVER.

3. *Cantor:* Great is God, known in all works of power.
ALL: (Repeat)
Cantor: Tell out God's glory for ever, hallelujah!
ALL: TELL OUT GOD'S GLORY FOR EVER, AND WORSHIP; etc.

4. *Cantor:* Praise your Lord brightly, loud-sounding trumpet;
    ALL: *(Repeat)*
    Cantor: flute and harp, heighten the music, hallelujah!
    ALL: FLUTE AND HARP, HEIGHTEN THE MUSIC AND
              WORSHIP; etc.

5. *Cantor:* Tambourines, keep the pulse in all our music;
    ALL: *(Repeat)*
    Cantor: beating drums, fill us with rhythm, hallelujah!
    ALL: BEATING DRUMS, FILL US WITH RHYTHM AND
              WORSHIP; etc.

6. *Cantor:* Melodies, blend your voices in beauty;
    ALL: *(Repeat)*
    Cantor: cymbals clash, banish all chaos, hallelujah.
    ALL: CYMBALS CLASH, BANISH ALL CHAOS, AND
              WORSHIP; etc.

7. *Cantor:* Clap and sing, praise God, now and for ever
    ALL: *(Repeat)*
    Cantor: while there's life, breath still remaining, hallelujah!
    ALL: WHILE THERE'S LIFE, BREATH STILL REMAINING, WE
              WORSHIP; etc.

This is a beautiful Pakistani song based on Psalm 150 which should be accompanied by nothing more than a tabla or drum.

After the introductory refrain, soloist and congregation share the verses in dialogue.

Although the tonality and text may seem strange at first, they are quickly assimilated and enjoyed.

This song is featured on the album ONE IS THE BODY.

Heaven on earth

Tune: 'HO RI HO RO', Alexander Sinclair.

THE GOD OF HEAVEN IS PRE - SENT ON EARTH IN

D   C   D

WORD AND SI - LENCE AND SHA - RING, IN FACE OF DOUBT, IN

A   D   D7   G   F#min

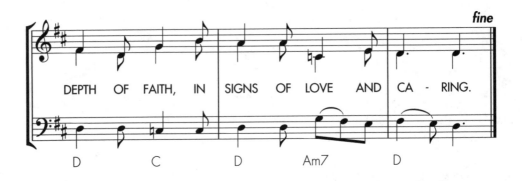

DEPTH OF FAITH, IN SIGNS OF LOVE AND CA - RING.

D   C   D   Am7   D

Tune: by Alexander Sinclair, copyright © The Sir Hugh Roberton Trust – Roberton Publications. Words and arrangement by John L. Bell and Graham Maule, copyright © 1988, 2001 WGRG, Iona Community, Glasgow, Scotland.

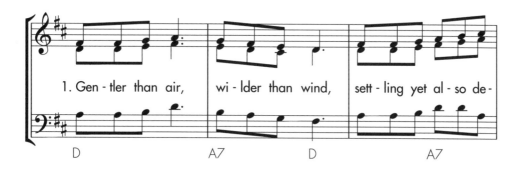

1. Gen - tler than air, wi - lder than wind, sett - ling yet al - so de-

D · A7 · D · A7

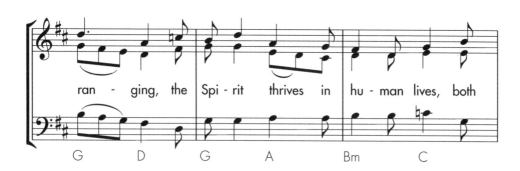

ran - ging, the Spi - rit thrives in hu - man lives, both

G · D · G · A · Bm · C

D.C.

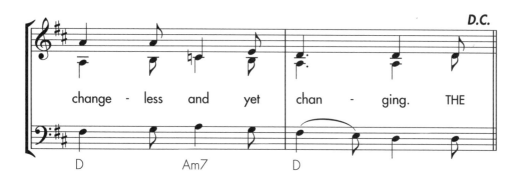

change - less and yet chan - ging. THE

D · Am7 · D

THE GOD OF HEAVEN IS PRESENT ON EARTH
IN WORD AND SILENCE AND SHARING,
IN FACE OF DOUBT, IN DEPTH OF FAITH,
IN SIGNS OF LOVE AND CARING.

1. Gentler than air, wilder than wind,
    settling yet also deranging,
    the Spirit thrives in human lives
    both changeless and yet changing.

2. Far from the church, outside the fold,
    where prayer turns feeble and nervous,
    the Spirit wills society's ills
    be healed through humble service.

3. From country quiet to city riots,
    in every human confusion,
    the Spirit pleads for all that leads
    to freedom from illusion.

4. Truth after tears, trust after fears,
    God making everyone wiser:
    the Spirit springs through hopeless things
    transforming what defies her.

Here we celebrate God's omnipresence or God's being everywhere on earth through the work of the Holy Spirit (female in Hebrew and Aramaic, male in Greek and English).

A simple three-part choral setting is offered of this very folkloristic tune which may be sung with a small music group singing the verses, or with everyone singing everything accompanied by guitar and flute or fiddle. Piano accompaniment deadens the song, the organ kills it. If neither flute nor guitar nor vocal trio is available, sing everything a capella.

This song is featured on the album ONE IS THE BODY.

I bow my knee in prayer

Tune: 'DUNNING', Scots traditional.

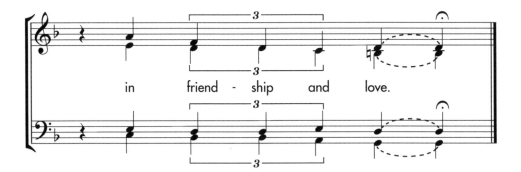

in friend - ship and love.

1. I bow my knee in prayer
    before the Father who made me,
    before the Son who purchased me,
    before the Spirit who cleansed me,
    in friendship and love.

2. Lord, through your anointed,
    give us the fullness we long for:
    love and affection for our God,
    the smile and wisdom of our God,
    the grace of God.

3. So may we live on earth
    as saints and angels in heaven;
    each shade and light, each day and night,
    through every moment we draw our breath,
    God, give us your Spirit.

Nobody knows how old either this text or tune is.

The words were gathered by a 19th-century scholar, Alexander Carmichael, from people in the Western Isles of Scotland. He translated them from Gaelic into English.

The origin of the tune is unknown. It may go far back in history or be a 19th-century composition.

Whatever the background, this song is a beautiful devotional text.

A choral arrangement of this text may be found in the GIA catalogue at G–5169. The song is featured on the album TAKE THIS MOMENT.

I owe my Lord a morning song

Tune: 'NAFZIGER', John L. Bell.

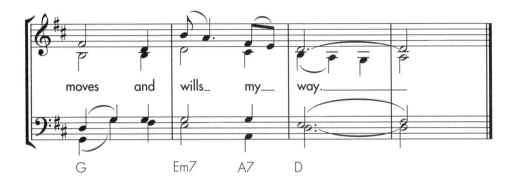

moves and wills_ my_ way._

G   Em7   A7   D

1. I owe my Lord a morning song
   for God has meant this day.
   Through fears of night and hidden light
   God moves and wills my way.

2. I owe my Lord a morning song
   for Jesus rose at dawn;
   he made death die and would not lie
   that others might live on.

3. I owe my Lord a morning song;
   the Spirit gave me voice;
   nor did she force my soul to praise
   but honoured me with choice.

4. I owe my Lord a morning song.
   How can I help but sing
   when God is all in all, and I
   am one with everything.

The genesis of this song was a conversation on the music of African–American spirituals between Ken Nafziger, a professor of music at the Eastern Mennonite University, and Pamela Warrick Smith, a celebrated exponent of African–American spirituals and work songs.

The text and tune reflect the passions of both people.

Single copies for choirs are available from the GIA catalogue at G–5164, and the song is featured in the collection TAKE THIS MOMENT.

Faithful, faithful is our God

(Ka mana 'o 'i 'o)

Tune: 'KA MANA 'O 'I 'O', Joe Camacho.

KA MANA 'O 'I 'O, O KO KĀKOU AKUA,
FAITHFUL, FAITHFUL IS OUR GOD. (Repeat)

1.   In love there is no one more faithful than our God,
       who brings the light into our darkness,
       the God who shares the breath of life in you and me,
       all living things upon the earth.

2.   In quiet moments God whispers tenderly
       the mystery of unending love;
       for God is good and holds us as we sleep
       then wakes us with the morning light.

3.   The mercy of our God is ours to share each day,
       to help each other on our way,
       to be God's hands and heart, God's tenderness and care,
       God's faithful people in the world.

The Hawaiian Islands were illegally seized by the USA at the end of the 19th century and made into a US state without the agreement of the people or their queen (who was imprisoned). Despite having a distinct language and a Pacific–Polynesian culture, native Hawaiians have fewer land rights than native American Indians.

This contemporary song, written by a parish musician on the Big Island, is typical of the warmth of the Hawaiian people and of their musical language.

It is best sung with a soloist taking the verse accompanied by guitar, and the congregation singing the chorus.

This song is featured on the album ONE IS THE BODY.

Here you are among us

(Tú estas presente)

Tune: Brazilian traditional.

Tú es - tas pre - sen - te, O Dios de'a - mor! Re - ve - ren - te-

Em   B7   Em7/D   C   B7   Em   B7

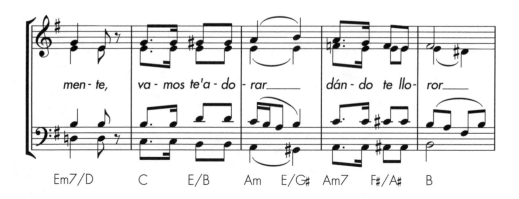

men - te, va - mos te'a - do - rar____ dán - do te llo - ror____

Em7/D   C   E/B   Am   E/G#   Am7   F#/A#   B

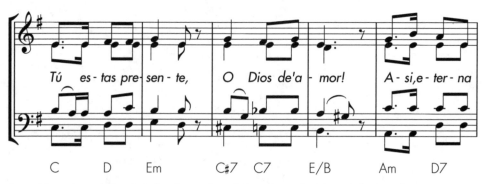

Tú es - tas pre - sen - te, O Dios de'a - mor! A - si,e - ter - na

C   D   Em   C#7   C7   E/B   Am   D7

Original Spanish words & melody Brazilian traditional. Arrangement by John L. Bell, copyright © 2002 WGRG, Iona Community, Glasgow, Scotland.

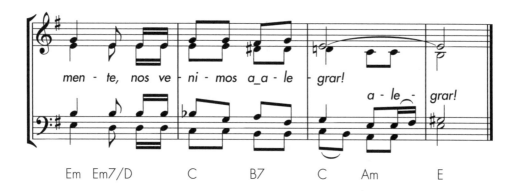

men - te, nos ve - ni - mos a_a - le - grar!

a - le - grar!

Em Em7/D   C   B7   C   Am   E

Tú estas presente, O Dios de amor!
reverentemente, vamos te adorar
dándo te lloror.
Tú estas presente, O Dios de amor!
Asi eternamente, nos venimos a alegrar!

Here you are among us, O God of love.
Reverently, we offer you our praise,
and offer you our sorrow.
Here you are among us, O God of love;
therefore we will praise you for ever.

This gentle Brazilian song which prepares us for worship can be sung repeatedly in the original or the English translation. It should either be accompanied by a four-part choir or a quiet keyboard instrument.

This song is featured on the album ONE IS THE BODY.

Be still, be silent

(Thula)

Tune: Swaziland traditional.

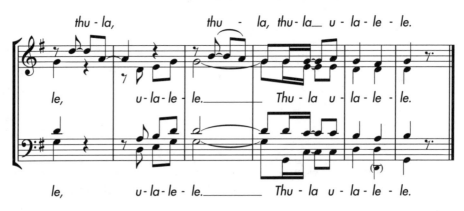

Thula, thula ulalele.

Be still, be silent.

Here is a very easy to sing song for the beginning or closing of worship, the speed varying according to the intention.

This song is featured on the album ONE IS THE BODY.

Chitra's tune

Tune: 'Chitra 1', Chitra Karki.

In a relaxed fashion ♩ = 50

Oh
Your king - dom come, Lord; may your will be
done, Lord, here on the earth as it is in
heaven. Your king - dom come, Lord; may your will be

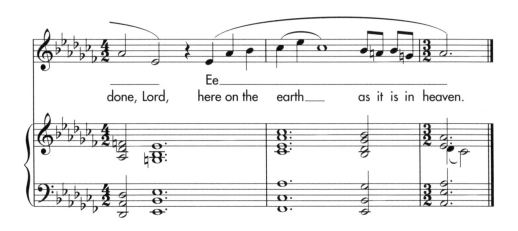

done, Lord,   here on the   earth____   as it is in heaven.

Chitra Karki is a Nepali evangelist and a friend of the Wild Goose Worship Group. He is largely responsible for an initiative to enable Christians in Nepal to hear and learn indigenous Christian songs through a tape ministry.

He personally has written a number of songs, but here a melodic fragment which he uses for meditation is included. There is no text. Chitra will simply change the vowel sound from 'aa' to 'ee' or 'o' as the mood takes him. However it is possible to use the following text:

> Your kingdom come, Lord;
> may your will be done, Lord,
> here on the earth
> as it is in heaven.

Alternatively, the chant may be sung interspersed with selected verses from the Psalms which are read over the accompaniment.

A psalm meditation using this music is featured on the album ONE IS THE BODY.

This is the day of rest

Tune: 'OLD DYSART', John L. Bell.

Brightly ♩ = 110

This is the day of rest, to use as God in - ten - ded:

time to re - new our faith and let our lives be men - ded;

time to ful - fil our song and time to re - dis -

co - ver those to whom we be -

long,   and   God who   is   our   lo - ver.

1. This is the day of rest,
   to use as God intended:
   time to renew our faith
   and let our lives be mended;
   time to fulfil our song
   and time to rediscover
   those to whom we belong,
   and God who is our lover.

2. Here is the feast of life
   to which we are invited;
   here Jesus offers food
   through which we are united:
   food for a company
   redeemed by blood and water,
   food through which God declares,
   'You are my son, my daughter.'

3. This is the time of change
   delivered by God's Spirit
   moving to life and health
   those claiming little merit;
   change which God's love demands
   to prove that faith is living,
   change which must overflow
   in justice and forgiving.

4. Glory to God on high,
   to Christ and to the Spirit.
   Glory to God on earth,
   whose image we inherit.
   Glory to God alone,
   our sacrament and story,
   in whom we live and move
   till lifted into glory.

The section concludes with a celebratory hymn for Sunday which is primarily intended for use when there is a eucharist or mass.

The People of God

Around the baptismal font in Clifton Cathedral, Bristol, is the statement:
Once you were no people;
now you are God's people.

The words come from the first letter of Peter, but their reference is not confined to those who have been baptised; rather the title of God's People is given to all those whom God, in Christ, has chosen to be his own. And since it was not simply to his own race, the Jews, that Jesus came, but equally to those outside the established religious communities, the title God's People is not exclusive.

Ultimately it is not we who award ourselves a new name on the basis of spiritual merit; it is God who has opted for us who calls us to belong to the community Christ initiated.

The Church from its origin has been diverse – in style of government, in forms of worship, and in membership. Bland uniformity was not one of the Pentecostal gifts of the Holy Spirit; diversity was – a rich diversity in which men and women, old and young, affluent and indigent interact with and belong to each other.

In this section, therefore, there are songs which indicate the wide range of our spiritual ancestors and contemporary companions in the Body of Christ.

Women and men as God intended

Tune: 'KOM NU MET ZANG' Netherlands traditional.

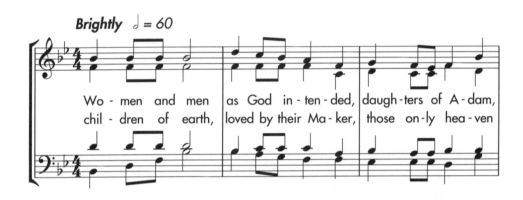

Wo - men and men | as God in - ten - ded, | daugh-ters of A - dam,
chil - dren of earth, | loved by their Ma - ker, | those on-ly hea - ven

sons of Eve; | yet in our lo - ving | we are not one with
could con - ceive; | |

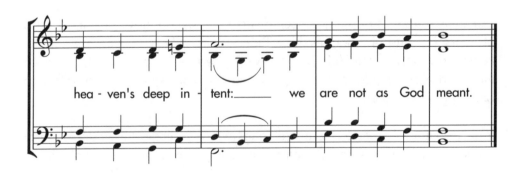

hea - ven's deep in - tent:____ we | are not as God | meant.

Words & arrangement by John L. Bell, copyright © 2002 WGRG, Iona Community, Glasgow, Scotland.

1. Women and men as God intended
daughters of Adam, sons of Eve;
children of earth, loved by their Maker,
those only heaven could conceive;
yet in our loving we are not one
with heaven's deep intent:
we are not as God meant.

2. Ours is the shame, ours is the story,
ours is a squandered legacy;
fallen from grace, fearful of glory,
lost is our true humanity.
How can the goodness heaven endowed
which earth cannot afford
be once again restored?

3. Into our world, born of a woman,
comes, in the flesh, the living God;
moved by our plight, suffering rejection,
feeling for those whose lives are flawed,
pardoning all who truly repent
comes Jesus Christ our Lord,
God's liberating Word.

4. Now sing aloud! Jesus our brother
turns every tide of history,
sharing our flesh, bearing our sorrow,
winning an endless liberty.
Out of the grave, alive in the world,
Christ wills all be made new:
this tested Word is true.

There should be little difficulty for people to pick up this traditional Dutch melody. It almost sings itself in the mouths of those who do not know it. For variety, men and women may take a middle verse each. However, to prevent the flawed association of women with the 'Fall', it is suggested that the men sing verse 2 and the women sing verse 3.

This song is featured on the album ONE IS THE BODY.

God it was

Tune: Scots Gaelic traditional (adapted).

Words & arrangement by John L. Bell & Graham Maule, copyright © 1989, 2002 WGRG, Iona Community, Glasgow, Scotland.

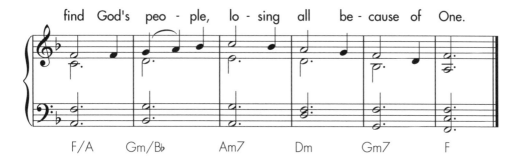

find God's peo - ple, lo - sing all be - cause of One.

F/A   Gm/Bb   Am7   Dm   Gm7   F

1. God it was who said to Abraham,
    'Pack your bags and travel on.'
    God it was who said to Sarah,
    'Smile and soon you'll bear a son.'
    Travelling folk and aged mothers
    wandering when they thought they'd done –
    this is how we find God's people,
    leaving all because of One.

2. God it was who said to Moses,
    'Save my people, part the sea.'
    God it was who said to Miriam,
    'Sing and dance to show you're free.'
    Shepherd-saints and tambourinists
    doing what God knew they could –
    this is how we find God's people,
    liberating what they should.

3. God it was who said to Joseph,
    'Down your tools and take your wife.'
    God it was who said to Mary,
    'In your womb, I'll start my life!'
    Carpenter and country maiden
    leaving town and trade and skills –
    this is how we find God's people,
    moved by what their Maker wills.

(continued)

4. Christ it was who said, 'Zacchaeus,
I would like to eat with you.'
Christ it was who said to Martha,
'Listening's what you need to do.'
Civil servants and housekeepers,
changing places at a cost –
this is how Christ summons people,
calling both the loved and lost.

5. In this crowd which spans the ages,
with these saints whom we revere,
God wants us to share their purpose
starting now and starting here.
So we celebrate our calling,
so we raise both heart and voice,
as we pray that through our living
more may find they are God's choice.

God it was is a song which celebrates the diversity of people whom God called and the often unusual nature of their calling.

It is a longish song. Five verses exhaust most people. It would therefore be helpful to alternate verses between men and women, or for verses 1 to 4 to have a soloist sing the first half and the congregation the second half, with all singing the final verse together.

The best accompaniment for this largely unknown island tune is a guitar and fiddle.

Gifts of the Spirit

Tune: 'PERSONENT HODIE', German traditional.

Steadily ♩ = 56

When our Lord walked the earth, all the world found its worth;

as de - clared at his birth God be - came our neigh - bour,

gran - ting us with fa - vour:

POWER TO SPEAK AND HEAL, GRACE TO

KNOW WHAT'S REAL, WIS - DOM, IN - SIGHT AND FAITH,

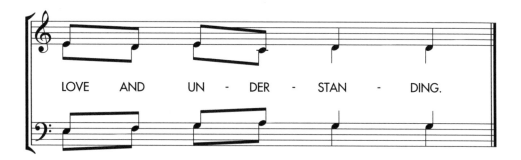

LOVE AND UN - DER - STAN - DING.

1. When our Lord walked the earth,
   all the world found its worth;
   as declared at his birth,
   God became our neighbour,
   granting us with favour

   POWER TO SPEAK AND HEAL,
   GRACE TO KNOW WHAT'S REAL,
   WISDOM, INSIGHT AND FAITH,
   LOVE AND UNDERSTANDING.

2. Through his life, through his death,
   through each gesture and breath,
   Jesus joined faith and deed,
   model for our caring,
   showing and yet sharing

3. Jesus loves all his friends
   and that love never ends;
   to his Church gifts he sends
   through the Holy Spirit.
   These we still inherit:

4. Sing and smile and rejoice,
   clap your hands, raise your voice;
   for, with unnerving choice,
   God, in Christ, has found us,
   and displays around us

Despite its title, this hymn is not exclusively pentecostal. Rather, it explores the gifts which the disciples of Jesus should expect to exhibit because of their commitment to him and his promise of the guidance of the Holy Spirit.

The tune is well known and frequently appears in four-part harmony and organ arrangements. This is a much simpler arrangement, allowing for the folk roots of the melody to be exposed. It should be sung a capella with a bodhrain or hand-drum accompanying.

This hymn is featured on the album ONE IS THE BODY.

To be a soldier

Tune: 'MILES CHRISTI', John L. Bell.

Maestoso ♩ = 80

To be a sol-dier, to fight for peace, till war shall end -

this is the con-flict Chri-st calls you to at - tend:

to for-feit safe - ty for dan-ger, and then, e - ven

stran-ger, turn e - ne - my to friend.

1. To be a soldier,
    to fight for peace till war shall end –
    this is the conflict
    Christ calls you to attend:
    to forfeit safety for danger
    and then, even stranger,
    turn enemy to friend.

2. To be a soldier
    confront more than the human foe;
    a greater struggle
    the cosmic Christ shall show:
    sin must be stripped
    from high places;
    what scars souls and faces
    he bids you overthrow.

3. To be a soldier
    means more than wishing war would cease:
    it calls for courage
    to bring the poor release,
    to enter politics praying
    and break rank obeying
    the power and Prince of peace.

4. Think not to weary
    or lay your great commission down;
    nor crave approval,
    nor fear the critic's frown.
    Prevail through tears, love with laughter,
    risk all and hereafter
    receive from Christ your crown.

This hymn commemorates the life of George Fielden MacLeod, holder of the Military Cross, minister of the Gospel, peer of the realm, pacifist, prophet and founder of the Iona Community. It was first sung at his memorial service in Govan Old Parish Church, Glasgow in September 1991.

There is a line of women

Tune: 'THE SEVEN JOYS OF MARY', English traditional.

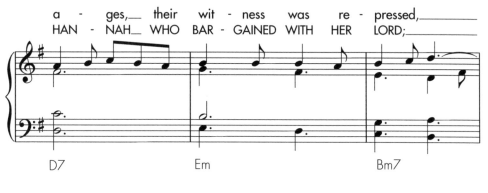

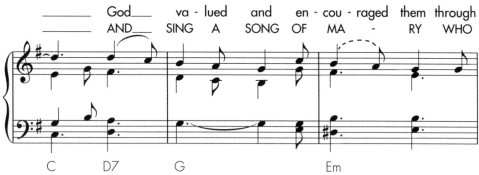

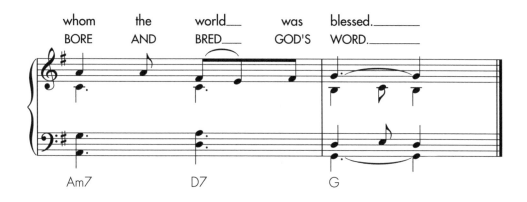

1. There is a line of women
   extending back to Eve
   whose role in shaping history
   God only could conceive.
   And though, through endless ages,
   their witness was repressed,
   God valued and encouraged them
   through whom the world was blessed.
   > So sing a song of Sarah
   > to laughter she gave birth;
   > and sing a song of Tamar
   > who stood for women's worth;
   > and sing a song of Hannah
   > who bargained with her Lord;
   > and sing a song of Mary
   > who bore and bred God's Word.

2. There is a line of women
   who took on powerful men
   defying laws and scruples
   to let life live again.
   And though, despite their triumph,
   their stories stayed untold
   God kept their number growing,
   creative, strong and bold.
   > So sing a song of Shiphrah
   > with Puah close at hand,
   > engaged to kill male children,
   > they foiled the king's command.
   > And sing a song of Rahab
   > who sheltered spies and lied;
   > and sing a song of Esther
   > preventing genocide.

3. There is a line of women
    who stood by Jesus' side,
    who housed him while he ministered
    and held him when he died.
    And though they claimed he'd risen
    their news was deemed suspect
    till Jesus stood among them,
    his womanly elect.
       So sing a song of Anna
       who saw Christ's infant face;
       and sing a song of Martha
       who gave him food and space;
       and sing of all the Marys
       who heeded his requests,
       and now at heaven's banquet
       are Jesus' fondest guests.

For many centuries, male preachers and denominational lectionaries have conspired to prevent the stories of biblical women or illustrations from the experience of contemporary women from being heard. Thus girls grow up in a church with few models of female discipleship, and boys presume that God's favoured gender is masculine.

This song reflects a few of the many stories of (subversive) women in the Bible.

It works best if a soloist sings the first half of the verse, and the whole assembly the second half as if it were a chorus.

This song is featured on the album ONE IS THE BODY.

We belong to God

(Somos del Señor)

Tune: Mexican, source unknown.

1. When we are living, we are in the Lord,
   and when we're dying, we are in the Lord;
   for in our living and in our dying
   we belong to God, we belong to God.

2. Each day allows us to decide for good,
   loving and serving as we know we should;
   in thankful giving, in hopeful living,
   we belong to God, we belong to God.

3. Sometimes we sorrow, other times we embrace,
   sometimes we question everything we face;
   yet in our yearning is deeper learning:
   we belong to God, we belong to God. *(continued)*

4. Till earth is over may we always know
love never fails us: God has made it so.
Hard times will prove us, never remove us;
we belong to God, we belong to God.

Pues si vivimos, para El vivimos,
y si morimos, para El morimos;
sea que vivamos o que moramos
somos del Señor, somos del Señor.

This is a beautiful Mexican song which indicates that our prime category of belonging is to God. It may be sung at services of baptism, confirmation or commitment or at funeral and memorial worship.

While the earth remains

Tune: 'ARIRAM', Korean, source unknown.

HAR - - VEST, SUM - MER SUN AND WIN - TER MOON, THE DEAD OF NIGHT, THE BRIGHT DAY.____

1. God, who made the earth, declared it good in the beginning,
   meant a time and purpose for all things that were and would be.

   > WHILE EARTH REMAINS
   > THERE WILL BE SEED TIME AND HARVEST,
   > SUMMER, SUN AND WINTER MOON,
   > THE DEAD OF NIGHT, THE BRIGHT DAY.

2. Though humanity defiled the Eden God had cherished,
   God did not despise the world whose worth its Maker could see.

3. So, in Christ God came from paradise to imperfection,
   repossessing earth and people through a tomb and a tree.

4. Wood, though felled to earth, produced a blossom none could perish;
   seed, though dead and fallen, burst to life and rose up again.

5. We, who follow Christ, discover heaven through limitation;
   pruned, we bear more fruit, and grafted to the Vine we are free.

(notes overleaf)

The tune to *While the earth remains* comes from Korea and is dearly loved by people from North and South. Its original text describes unrequited love between two people, a metaphor for the yearning which exists in a divided nation.

It would have been impossible to provide a relevant English language version suitable for congregational song. Instead the above text points to the resolution and fulfilment of all things in Christ.

The song may be sung with soloist and congregation alternating verse and chorus.

A choral arrangement of this song is found in the GIA catalogue at G–5160, and a recording of the same is featured on the album TAKE THIS MOMENT.

Because the Saviour prayed

Tune: 'ATHAIR UILE-CHUMHACHDAICH', Alasdair Codona.

1. Because the Saviour prayed that we be one
   and taught his friends to say, 'Your will be done',
   we sense God's call as in God's sight we dare
   commit ourselves in answer to Christ's prayer.

2. Our narrow loyalties have had their day –
   these separate ways, demeaning Christ the Way;
   we own the sorry scars that paved the past,
   yet gladly seek the road God made to last.

3. We are our Saviour's body, Christ the head,
   first born of God, first risen from the dead.
   Dismembered, we debase his holy will;
   united, his intention we fulfil.

4. So guide us, Lord, and take us by the hand,
   and show us how to love and understand;
   reveal, within the differences we share,
   the pattern of your glory, grace and care.

5. And when our journey here has reached its end
   and strangers are the pilgrims you intend,
   may we, with gratitude for all you've given,
   enjoy you in the harmony of heaven.

This hymn was written for the inauguration of the Council of Churches in Britain and Ireland, which took place in the Anglican and Roman Catholic cathedrals in Liverpool in May 1990.

The text draws on various references in the Gospels and the New Testament Letters which indicate God's desire for unity and yet for difference. It is most appropriately used at ecumenical occasions.

Alternative tunes are 'Woodlands' and 'Sursum Corda'.

O God, you made us all unique

Tune: 'PRIVILEGE', John L. Bell.

1. O God, you made us all unique;
    one pattern for each life you found.
    Where falling short of your design
    you see us, free us
    till by love we're bound.

2. O Christ, you summon into life
    our timid faith, our hidden skill.
    Where trust or talent are untried,
    there tend us. Send us
    grace to know your will.

3. O Holy Spirit, breath of life,
    our noblest visions you inspire.
    Where hearts are cold or minds are dull,
    there shake us. Make us
    flames of heaven's fire.

4. To God, in whom we live and move,
    we vow our love and loyalty;
    and here ascribe all honour, power
    and glory, glory
    now and endlessly.

It may be best for the first three verses of this song to be sung solo, possibly by different people, with the congregation joining in the last verse. That way, there should be no need to teach the tune in advance.

Maker and Mover

Tune: 'MAKER AND MOVER', John L. Bell.

1. Maker and Mover, Light and Life,
   God of eternity,
   you, with enchantment, crafted the world
   and intended me.

2. Sun in its shining, wind in chase,
   sea in its restless wave
   witness your beauty, wonder and skill
   none can slight or save.

3. Born of this beauty, Jesus came,
   sent for the world to see
   purpose and person, God in the raw,
   true humanity.

4. Not all were happy, hallowed, healed;
   not all he called agreed;
   yet, in the mystery, people like me
   found he knew my need.

5. To what you call me, though unknown,
   Lord, let my life say Yes,
   finding how those who don't know it all
   are the folk you bless.

6. Then, in my following, in my faith,
   in what I fail or prove,
   let me be true to you and to me
   and to all I love.

Though this is a personal song of commitment, it is also illustrative of the engagement of God with humanity at large and the disciple in particular.

God's Spirit is here

Tune: 'OLD 104th', Genevan.

God's Spi-rit is here that ne-ver a - lone the fol-lowers of Christ need face the un-known. The fount of all li-ving is lea-ding the dance, dis-man-tling old sys-tems that

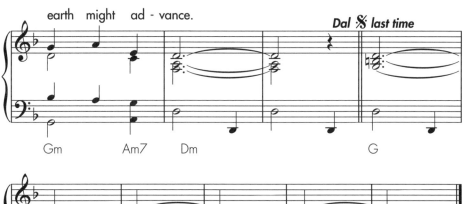
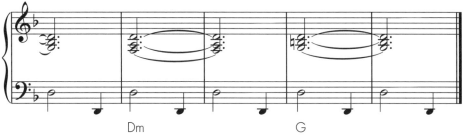

1. God's Spirit is here
    that never alone
    the followers of Christ
    need face the unknown.
    The fount of all living
    is leading the dance,
    dismantling old systems
    that earth might advance.

2. She banishes sin,
    eradicates fear,
    lets hesitant faith
    affirm God is here,
    till, living like Jesus
    and blessed by his name,
    we bind up the broken
    and lift up the lame.

3. She defuses hate
    and raises the dead,
    becalming life's storms
    removing all dread.
    So that we might serve God,
    confirmed from above,
    she tests us with fire
    and aflames us with love.

4. So, seek out the lost,
    and share out the pain,
    and love at such cost
    that all rise aqain.
    God's lamplighting spirit
    is dancing the way
    through dark into dawning,
    from night into day.

(notes overleaf)

God's spirit is here is adapted from a Litany used in a theological college in Bangalore. As with other songs relating to the activity of the Holy Spirit, the third person of the Trinity is referred to in the feminine – which is perfectly consonant with Hebrew and Aramaic language.

The tune is an ancient Genevan psalm tune, normally sung slowly and in four-part harmony. This arrangement allows its possible folk or dance origins to be celebrated.

We rejoice to be God's chosen

Tune: 'NETTLETON', American traditional.

With a spring ♩ = 100

We re-joice to be God's cho-sen, not through vir-tue, work, or

skill, but be-cause God's love is gene-rous, un-con-formed to hu-man

will. And be-cause God's love is rest - less like the

sur - ging of the sea, we are pulled by heaven's dy -

nam - ic to be - come, not just to be.

1. We rejoice to be God's chosen
   not through virtue, work or skill,
   but because God's love is generous,
   unconformed to human will.
   And because God's love is restless,
   like the surging of the sea,
   we are pulled by heaven's dynamic
   to become, not just to be.

2. We rejoice to be God's chosen,
   to be gathered to God's side,
   not to build a pious ghetto
   or be steeped in selfish pride;
   but to celebrate the goodness
   of the One who sets us free
   from the smallness of our vision
   to become, not just to be.

3. We rejoice to be God's chosen,
   to align with heaven's intent,
   to await where we are summoned
   and accept where we are sent.
   We rejoice to be God's chosen
   and, amidst all that we see,
   to anticipate with wonder
   that the best is yet to be.

At first, the sentiment of this text may seem presumptuous and even arrogant, until we accept that what we delight and boast in is not our own goodness but the unnerving grace of God in choosing us.

The tune is a fine old American melody, probably with roots in Britain or Ireland. It is best sung a capella and in unison.

A choral concertato version of this hymn is found in the GIA catalogue at G –5171, and is featured on the album TAKE THIS MOMENT.

The Word of God

Devout Christians always run the risk of being either idolators or bibliolators. The first temptation comes from believing that our theology is the only theology and thus God ends up being little bigger than our imagination. The second happens when the Bible is held to be an unquestionable icon rather than the book through which God wishes to engage us in a relationship.

It is precisely because both theology and an unhealthy doctrine of scripture failed that the Word became flesh.

However, in this section we deal primarily with how biblical texts may be sung – a practice which is older than Christianity, given that Jesus participated in singing the psalms.

Most psalm texts in this collection are offered in a metrical version, that being the form favoured by both Reformed and Anglican churches after the Reformation.

Keep me, Lord

Tune: 'MIKTAM', John L. Bell.

Paraphrase (of Psalm 16) & music by John L. Bell, copyright © 2002 WGRG, Iona Community, Glasgow, Scotland.

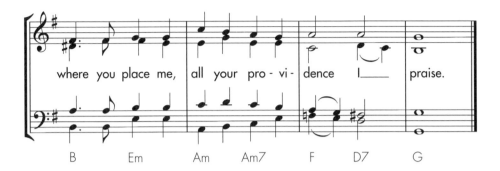

where you place me, all your pro-vi-dence I___ praise.

B   Em   Am   Am7   F   D7   G

1. Keep me, Lord, for in your keeping
I have found security,
and, rejoicing in your presence,
know and own my destiny.
You, my Lord, my cup, my portion,
plot my lifeline, chart my days;
well content with where you place me,
all your providence I praise.

2. I shall bless the Lord for giving
sound advice for broad daylight;
wisdom for my inmost being
God communicates by night.
So I set the Lord before me
holding fast to each command;
disregarding what dares shake me,
God I keep at my right hand.

3. Therefore body, mind and spirit
in serenity abound;
death and hell can never menace
those whose faith in God is found.
You, O gracious Lord, will show me
paths to all you have in store:
in your presence, in your purpose,
pleasures last for evermore.

Psalm 16 celebrates the trust we can have in God whose care for us is constant. This setting is ideal for four-part choral singing.

A recording of this psalm setting is featured in the album ONE IS THE BODY.

I will always bless the Lord

Tune: 'TALLA CRIOSDH', Scots Gaelic traditional.

Paraphrase (of Psalm 34) & arrangement by John L. Bell, copyright © 1997 WGRG, Iona Community, Glasgow, Scotland.

1. I will always bless the Lord,
   praise his name and love his word.
   Humble folk will fill with joy,
   as in God I glory.

2. When I prayed, God answered me,
   from my fears he set me free;
   none who trust God's faithful love
   shall be disappointed.

3. Those who cry are listened to,
   those in need receive their due;
   angels guard God's loyal folk,
   keeping them from danger.

4. Taste and see that God is good,
   know your yearnings understood,
   find your true security,
   be God's holy people.

5. *(Spoken over hummed melody by solo voice)*
   Princes may suffer hardship
   and go hungry,
   but those who wait on the Lord
   shall lack no good thing.

6. Alleluia,
   alleluia,
   alleluia,
   alleluia.

This psalm of confidence has deep significance for Celtic peoples. It is believed that St Columba of Iona, for whom copying scriptural manuscripts was a life-long activity, finished writing out the text of verse 10 shortly before he died.

Hence, it is suggested that in this setting, which goes to an ancient Gaelic lullabye, the penultimate verse is hummed as Columba's final text is spoken, following which all sing 'Alleluia' in unison.

The three-part setting is extremely easy to teach. All women should learn the tune, half the men sing the descending 'Alleluia', the other half hum on the bass note.
The psalm should be sung a capella thus:

verse 1: solo,   4: add tenor,
    2: women,   5: all hum harmony with a voice speaking the text,
    3: add bass drone,   6: all sing in unison.

This psalm is featured on the album ONE IS THE BODY.

Do not be vexed

Tune: 'HOUSE OF THE RISING SUN', Irish traditional.

Paraphrase (of Psalm 37) & arrangement by John L. Bell, copyright © 1998 WGRG, Iona Community, Glasgow, Scotland.

1. Do not be vexed or envy
    those obsessed with doing wrong.
    Their fortune is like fields of grass
    whose growth cannot last long.

2. Trust in the Lord, do what is right;
    take root in God's good ground.
    Delight in God, for in God's will
    your heart's desire is found.

3. Give God your trust, and let the Lord
    direct your future way.
    The justice of your cause shall rise
    and shine as clear as day.

4. Do not be jealous or dismayed
    should evil folk succeed.
    wait patiently for God who comes
    in quietness to your need.

5. Better the pennies of the poor
    than wicked people's gain.
    God breaks their power, but humble folk
    will never live in vain.

In Psalm 37, the writer is dealing with a sense of dispiritedness felt when the wicked appear to prosper and the godly appear to have a hard time. In such a situation, the disciple is encouraged to stand firm and not be tempted to invest in wickedness. People who were around in the 1960s will recognise this tune as one of the standards for every budding guitarist. Its secular text probably came with the tune from Ireland to North America at the end of the 19th century. The tune, in the Dorian Mode, is very strong and worthy of more frequent singing.

A choral concertato version of this psalm is found in the GIA choral catalogue at G–4668 and is featured on the album PSALMS OF DAVID AND SONGS OF MARY.

Create within me a clean heart

Tune: 'CLEAN HEART', Alison Adam.

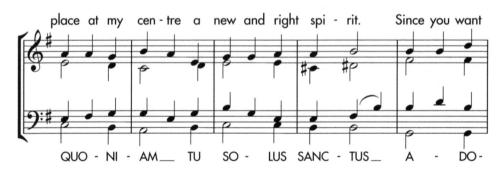

Paraphrase (of Psalm 51) & melody © 2001 Alison Adam. Arrangement by John L. Bell, copyright © 2001 WGRG, Iona Community, Glasgow, Scotland.

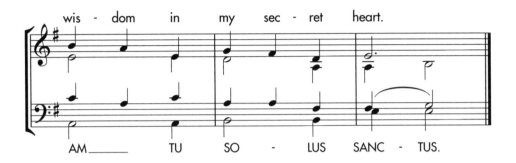

Create within me a clean heart, O God;
place at my centre a new and right spirit.
Since you want truth in my innermost being,
teach me your wisdom in my secret heart.

ADORAMUS DOMINE, QUONIAM TU SOLUS SANCTUS.
(We worship you, Lord, for you alone are holy.)

This is a meditative chant or response which can be sung repeatedly as a preparation for worship or as a response after a reading.

If sung in four-part harmony, let the first singing feature the sopranos singing the text and the others humming. Then the tenor joins and subsequently alto and bass sing the Latin text.

O Great God and Lord of the earth

Tune: 'VOS SOS EL DESTAZADO', El Salvador, source unknown.

1. O great God and Lord of the earth,
    rouse yourself and demonstrate justice;
    give the arrogant what they deserve,
    silence all malevolent boasting.
    > See how some you love are broken
    > for they know the weight of oppression;
    > even widows and orphans are murdered
    > and poor strangers are innocent victims.

2. Those who crush your people delight,
    claiming God above takes no notice;
    they proclaim that heaven is blind,
    that the God of Jacob is silent.
    > Stupid fools, when will you listen?
    > Now take heed, you ignorant people.
    > God who gave us sight and hearing
    > has observed and noted what happened.

3. God the Lord will not stay away
    nor forsake his well-beloved people;
    heaven's justice soon will appear
    and the pure in heart will embrace it.
    > Yes, the ones whom God instructed,
    > who revere and study God's word
    > will be saved from all that harms them
    > while a pit is dug for the wicked.

4. Should the wrong change places with right
    and the courts play host to corruption;
    should the innocent fear for their lives
    while the guilty smile at their scheming;
    > still the Lord will be your refuge,
    > be your strength and courage and tower.
    > Though your foot should verge on slipping,
    > God will cherish, keep and protect you.

As a result of the interest in Liberation Theology which emanated from Latin America, many people became familiar with *campesino* mass settings from Nicaragua and El Salvador in which the plea for God's justice to be visited on political and economic oppression was explicit. The language used was highly reminiscent of some of the protest psalms, of which Psalm 94 is an example, here set to a Salvadorean tune. The piece is best sung accompanied by a guitar.

This song is featured on the album ONE IS THE BODY.

Know that God is good

(Mungu ni mwema)

Tune: Democratic Republic of Congo, source unknown.

Proudly ♩ = 80

Mu - ngu ni mwe - ma. Mu - ngu
Know that God is good. Know that
Ha - le, ha - le - lu - ya. Ha - le,

ni mwe - ma. Mu - ngu ni mwe - ma,
God is good. Know that God is good,
Ha - le - lu - ya. Ha - le, ha - le - lu - ya,

ni mwe - ma, ni mwe - ma.
God is good, God is good.
Ha - le - lu - ya, ha - le - lu - ya.

Mungu ni mwema.

Know that God is good.

Hale, haleluya.

This African worship song is easily taught and remembered in four-part harmony. It may be used in response to the reading of the Bible, in prayers of gratitude or as a recessional. Both Swahili and English texts may be sung. Words from Psalm 100:3.

In deep distress

Tune: 'SHAPIRO', John L. Bell.

sessed your sight, Lord, who'd es-cape dam - na - tion?'

1. In deep distress my soul declares
   its song of lamentation:
   'Lord, hear my voice.
   Your listening ear determines my salvation.
   If human guilt was your delight
   and sin alone obsessed your sight,
   Lord, who'd escape damnation.'

2. Though punishment should be our prize,
   another gift is given;
   for pardon is your property,
   the greatest grace of heaven.
   We fear your love more than your might
   because you exercise the right to name
   our sins forgiven.

3. So now my soul in penitence
   affirms the hope I stand on.
   Like those who wait to see the dawn,
   I yearn to know your pardon.
   No power can weaken or deform
   God's will to challenge and transform,
   abase but not abandon.

Psalm 130, the 'De Profundis' is one of the best known of the psalms which express personal despair and affirm a belief in God's grace.

For best effect, let a soloist take the first verse to establish the singularity of voice, then v. 2 may be sung in unison and v. 3 in harmony.

A three- and four-part choral setting of this psalm is available in the GIA catalogue, G–5167, and is featured on the album TAKE THIS MOMENT.

Listen now for the Gospel

(Yakanaka Vhangeri)

Tune: Zimbabwean traditional.

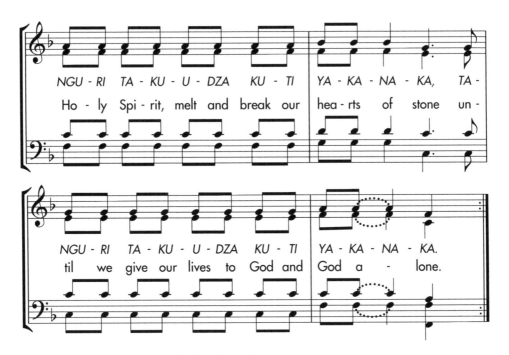

NGU - RI TA - KU - U - DZA KU - TI YA - KA - NA - KA, TA -
Ho - ly Spi - rit, melt and break our hea - rts of stone un -

NGU - RI TA - KU - U - DZA KU - TI YA - KA - NA - KA.
til we give our lives to God and God a - lone.

Cantor: Listen now for the Gospel;
ALL: ALLELUIA!
Cantor: It is God's word that changes us;
ALL: ALLELUIA! *(Repeat)*

1. *Cantor:* Come, Holy Spirit, melt and break our hearts of stone
    until we give our lives to God and God alone.
    ALL: COME, HOLY SPIRIT, MELT AND BREAK
    OUR HEARTS OF STONE
    UNTIL WE GIVE OUR LIVES TO GOD AND GOD ALONE.

2. *Cantor:* Come, Holy Spirit, root in us God's living word,
    that we may show the faithfulness of Christ our Lord.
    ALL: *(Repeat)*

3. *Cantor:* Come, Holy Spirit, bind the broken, find the lost,
    confirm in us the fire and love of Pentecost.
    ALL: *(Repeat)*

Original Shona text:
    Yakanaka Vhangeri,
    YAKANAKA! (Repeat)
    TANGURI TAKUUDZA KUTI YAKANAKA. (Repeat)

The literal translation of *Listen now for the Gospel* is:
    The Gospel is good!
    We have already told you. It is good!

In the original, the whole congregation sings the verse, the Cantor's part being confined to the chorus.

This version allows for the possibility of the song enhancing the hearing of the Gospel if it is sung before the Gospel is read.

I will arise

Tune: 'I WILL ARISE', John L. Bell.

1. I will arise and go to my father,
   come to my senses, confess what I've done;
   I will implore his peace and his pardon:
   all will be well and all be one.

2. I will arise and watch at the window,
   wait to recover and welcome my child;
   I will prepare a feast in his honour:
   all will be well and all be one.

3. I will arise and bury my envy,
   stretch out my hand to the one I have scorned;
   I will lay down the resentment I harbour:
   all will be well and all be one.

4. I will arise and go to my father;
   I will arise and welcome my child;
   I will lay down the resentment I harbour:
   all will be well and all be one.

The parable of the Prodigal Son involves three distinct people – the younger son, the father and the older brother. At different times in our lives we may identify with the actions of each of the characters.

In this song, based on the Gospel text in Luke 15:11–32, the three characters tell, as it were, their inside story. It may therefore be best to have each of the first three verses sung after the appropriate verses from scripture, with all singing the fourth verse. A hummed choral or keyboard accompaniment can undergird the text.

This song is featured on the album ONE IS THE BODY.

One is the body

Tune: 'PEACOCK', John L. Bell.

Moderato ♩ = 88

1. One is the bo - dy and one is the Head,
one is the Spi - rit by whom we are led;
one God and Fa - ther, one faith and one

Paraphrase (of Ephesians 4:11–16) & music by John L. Bell, copyright © 1997, 2002 WGRG, Iona Community, Glasgow, Scotland, and the Baptist Union of Great Britain & Ireland.

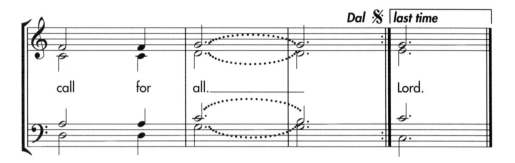

1. One is the body and one is the Head,
    one is the Spirit by whom we are led;
    one God and Father,
    one faith and one call for all.

2. Christ who ascended to heaven above
    is the same Jesus whose nature is love,
    who once descended
    to bring to this earth new birth.

3. Gifts have been given well suited to each;
    some to be prophets, to pastor or preach,
    some, through the Gospel,
    to challenge, convert and teach.

4. Called to his service are women and men
    so that his body might ever again
    witness through worship,
    through deed and through word
    to Christ our Lord.

The title of this collection comes from this song, a paraphrase of Ephesians 4:11–16 written for the 1997 Assembly of the Baptist Union of Great Britain and Ireland.

There is nothing complex about the melody but, in teaching, ensure that the congregation sings the E in bar 11, as the F in the bass sometimes throws people if it is over-emphasised.

The introduction may also be played as an interlude between verses.

This song is featured on the album ONE IS THE BODY.

Love one another

Tune: 'EWALRY' John L. Bell.

Paraphrase (of 1 John 4:7–19) & music by John L. Bell and Graham Maule, copyright © 2000 WGRG, Iona Community, Glasgow, Scotland.

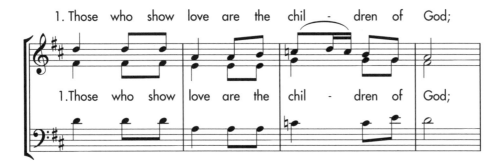

LOVE ONE ANOTHER FOR LOVE IS OF GOD.
THOSE WHO LIVE IN LOVE, LIVE IN GOD,
AND GOD LIVES IN THEM. *(Repeat)*

1. Those who show love are the children of God;
   father and mother is God to each of them.

2. God showed his love in the face of the Son;
   Christ lives in us so that we might live in him.

3. Love has no place for the menace of fear;
   fear is abandoned where perfect love is found.

4. Love has its purpose in God's holy will;
   we learn to love from the one who loved us first.

The First Letter of John is a bit of a jumble, seeming to move suddenly from one subject to another and to repeat itself. But throughout is the desire that love should bind the Christian community together. The fourth chapter is most precise about this.

The refrain is best sung by all with a trio taking the verses. For verses 2–4 the choral arrangement should be consulted.

A choral arrangement of this song is found in the GIA catalogue at G–5158, and is featured on the album TAKE THIS MOMENT.

Love is the touch

Tune: 'AMOR DEI', John L. Bell.

1. Love is the touch of in-tan-gi-ble joy;
love is the force that no fear can des-troy;
love is the good-ness we glad-ly ap-plaud:
God is where love is, for love is of God.

1. Love is the touch of intangible joy;
   love is the force that no fear can destroy;
   love is the goodness we gladly applaud:
   God is where love is, for love is of God.

2. Love is the lilt in a lingering voice;
   love is the hope that can make us rejoice;
   love is the cure for the frightened and flawed:
   God is where love is, for love is of God.

3. Love is the light in the tunnel of pain;
   love is the will to be whole once again;
   love is the trust of a friend on the road:
   God is where love is, for love is of God.

4. Love is the Maker and Spirit and Son;
   love is the kingdom their will has begun;
   love is the path which the saints all have trod:
   God is where love is, for love is of God.

In 1998, the major Christian traditions in Scotland co-operated in the production of an ecumenical supplement to their denominational hymnals. It was entitled *Common Ground*, and it included items by hitherto unpublished Scottish writers, one of whom is Alison Robertson.

Her text is more of a meditation than a paraphrase of the passage in 1 John cited above, and makes a good hymn for wedding or general use.

Commitment to God

Those who have gathered for worship, who have acknowledged their identity and belonging, who have listened for the word of God in the scripture and through each other cannot remain neutral.

Worship is not all about convictions, even the most noble and sound convictions. In worship God engages with us in order to change us. And our openness to being changed in body, mind and spirit is expressed in what we commit ourselves, under God, to do.

So, in this final section we have hymns and songs which enable us to rehearse how we will live as those who have encountered the living God, hymns through which we may claim God's blessing and commit ourselves at the end of the liturgy or the end of the day into God's care.

Ageless God

Tune: 'HOLY MANNA', John L. Bell.

1. Ageless God of boundless wonder,
    endless source of peerless grace,
    who, to shatter speculation,
    came incarnate face to face;
    you we praise, almighty Maker,
    Parent of humanity,
    Power behind the powers we cherish,
    Lord of life as life should be.

2. None among us stood attentive
    when you brought the world to birth,
    nor can any claim full knowledge
    of the future states of earth.
    Fascinated, still we struggle
    to make sense of what has been,
    and with differing dreams imagine
    what, as yet, remains unseen.

3. Each idea still gestating,
    each conviction in its youth,
    each encounter, each engagement,
    each impassioned search for truth –
    these we offer, not for blessing,
    but for shaping to your will.
    Here, good Lord, inspire, amaze us,
    fire our insight, fuse our skill.

4. Train our science to be servant
    of the needs we must perceive;
    teach our intellects, where blinded,
    that to see we must believe;
    in our politics prevent us
    from confusing means and ends;
    and through faith and doubt direct us
    to pursue what Christ intends.

At the end of the book of Job, God calls Job to account. Having at length and in earnest pondered the mystery of suffering, God confronts Job with another mystery – that of providence. And after God has asked Job questions about this mystery, Job falls silent.

That biblical encounter is the genesis of this hymn in which we both ponder the immensity of God's creativity and ask for God's guidance in what we learn and what we do with the world we live in.

116 All the wonder that surrounds us

Tune: 'AR HYD Y NOS', Welsh traditional.

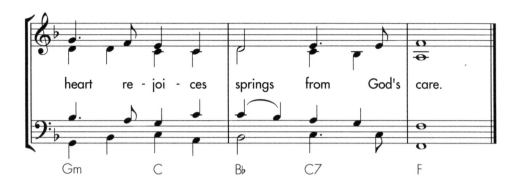

heart   re - joi - ces   springs   from   God's   care.

Gm   C   Bb   C7   F

1. All the wonder that surrounds us
    springs from God's care:
    all that marvels or confounds us,
    raw, rich or rare;
    touch and texture, sights and voices,
    nature's countless forms and choices:
    all for which the heart rejoices
    springs from God's care.

2. Every creature, every human
    lives by God's grace:
    every family, man and woman,
    culture and race;
    those whom fortune seems to favour,
    those exploited for their labour,
    those who need to know a neighbour
    live by God's grace.

3. How can we revere God's goodness
    meant for all time?
    How ensure that each uniqueness
    keeps in its prime?
    How can we revere with pleasure
    all God gives for life and leisure,
    how preserve each earthly treasure
    meant for all time?   *(continued)*

4. God has willed that peace and justice
walk hand in hand.
These, with love, shall build foundations
on which we'll stand:
love for lover, friend and stranger,
love defying death and danger,
love as first born in a manger –
heaven close at hand.

The care of creation as distinct from praise for creation has not been a prominent theme in Christian hymnody. But as we discover that humanity is threatened by ecological negligence as keenly as by nuclear bombing there is an urgency to offer to God committed prayer for the well-being of the earth. Our response should not be a knee-jerk reaction which comes from guilt but an intention to act which is the natural result of prayerful appreciation of what God created long before humanity could name its Maker.

This hymn is featured on the album ONE IS THE BODY.

You are the God of new beginnings

Tune: 'OTAGO ST', John L. Bell.

1. You are the God of new beginnings;
   you bless and free us from the past,
   and when its grip is long forgotten,
   your touch will last.

2. You are the God of second chances;
   though all the world declares we're done,
   your love restores us then invites us
   to rise and run.

3. You are the God of great tomorrows,
   brighter than all our yesterdays.
   Your heaven dwarfs our former glory,
   its promise stays.

4. You are the Alpha and Omega,
   our source of life and journey's end,
   and through the changes that you call us
   remain our friend.

5. Then let your Holy Spirit lead us
   as we, attentive to your word,
   achieve more than we dare imagine
   through Christ our Lord.

This is a simple song of commitment which may have its first four verses sung solo with the whole assembly joining in the final verse.

In concrete, brick and living stone

Tune: 'DAY OF REST'.

Words & arrangement by John L. Bell & Graham Maule, copyright © 2002 WGRG, Iona Community, Glasgow, Scotland.

1. In concrete, brick and living stone
    God builds a trysting place,
    a sign of contradicting love,
    an earth and heaven space.

2. Here, as the doors remain ajar,
    the city's cry and care
    inform God's worship that earth's work
    needs justice joined to prayer.

3. Thus, when his friends meet in his name,
    Christ's summons comes to each;
    some shield the poor, some share their wealth,
    some protest, heal or preach.

4. On these and on their work is sent
    God's Spirit, breath and flame,
    inspiring each to face the world
    and set on it Christ's claim.

5. Then, Lord, come now to where I stand
    that, grand though words may be,
    your kingdom may take flesh and root
    in this place and in me.

This was originally a hymn for an ordination in the city of Birmingham. However, its application is much wider and it is suitable for the general commitment of individuals or a congregation to their mission and ministry.

Sisters and brothers, with one voice

Tune: 'VULPIUS', 1609, German traditional.

Sis - ters and bro - thers, with one voice con - firm your cal - ling

and re - joice: each is God's child and each God's choice.

AL - LE - LU - IA! AL - LE - LU - IA! AL - LE - LU - IA!

Words & arrangement by John L. Bell & Graham Maule, copyright © 2002 WGRG, Iona Community, Glasgow, Scotland.

1. Sisters and brothers with one voice
   confirm your calling and rejoice:
   each is God's child and each God's choice.
   ALLELUIA! ALLELUIA! ALLELUIA!

2. Strangers no more, but cherished friends,
   live as the body God intends,
   sharing the love the Spirit sends.

3. Not, though, by wisdom, wealth or skill,
   nor by ourselves can we fulfil
   what, for the world, is God's own will.

4. Christ is the way. By him alone,
   seeds of the kingdom's life are sown,
   patterns of heaven and earth are shown.

5. Then follow him through every day.
   Fear not what crowds or critics say:
   those on the move stir those who stay.

6. In factory, office, home or hall;
   where people struggle, strive or stall,
   seek out and serve the Lord of All.

7. Seeking and serving, with one voice,
   confirm your calling and rejoice:
   each is God's child and each God's choice.

The stirring and sturdy tune 'Vulpius' enables this hymn as a recessional. Harmony is only offered for the chorus as when the verse is sung or played in harmony, the tune tends to drag. It should therefore be sung with verve and perhaps accompanied by a bodhrain or hand-drum and a flute or whistle.

Take this moment

Tune: 'TAKE THIS MOMENT', John L. Bell.

Gently and quietly ♩ = ca. 86

1. Take this mo - ment, sign__ and__ space,

1. Take this moment, sign and space;
   take my friends around;
   here among us make the place
   where your love is found.

2. Take the time to call my name,
   take the time to mend
   who I am and what I've been,
   all I've failed to tend.

3. Take the tiredness of my days,
   take my past regret,
   letting your forgiveness touch
   all I can't forget.

4. Take the little child in me
   scared of growing old;
   help me here to find my worth
   made in Christ's own mould.

5. Take my talents, take my skills,
   take what's yet to be;
   let my life be yours, and yet
   let it still be me.

This is a song for personal commitment and can be sung solo throughout or with the whole assembly joining in the last verse.

A choral and instrumental arrangement of this song is available in the GIA Catalogue, G–5166, and is featured on the album TAKE THIS MOMENT.

I'll praise eternal God

(Je lourai l'Éternel)

Tune: 'JE LOURAI L'ÉTERNEL', French, source unknown.

Original words & melody French, source unknown © copyright control. Translation & arrangement by John L. Bell, copyright © 2002 WGRG, Iona Community, Glasgow, Scotland.

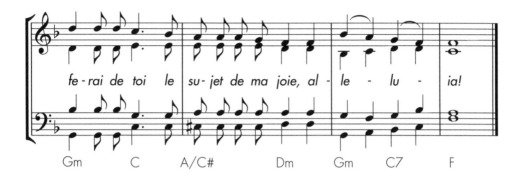

fe - rai de toi le su - jet de ma joie, al - le - lu - ia!

Gm   C   A/C#   Dm   Gm   C7   F

Je louerai l'Éternel de tout mon coeur,
je raconterai toutes tes merveilles,
je chanterai ton nom.
Je louerai l'Éternel de tout mon coeur,
je ferai de toi le sujet de ma joie, alleluia!

I'll praise eternal God with all my heart,
and I will recount your marvellous works
and glorify your name.
I'll praise eternal God with all my heart.
I'll make you, my Lord, the subject of my joy. Alleluia!

There are some songs which just don't sound right in English. This is one of them. A metrical translation is offered, but it is suggested that the French is sung, to acknowledge both that God favours no human mother-tongue and that the Church is intentionally international.

We will walk with God

(Sizohamba)

Tune: Swaziland traditional.

till the king - dom has come.
si - zo - ham - ba na - ye.

Sizohamba naye,
wo wo wo,
sizohamba naye. (Repeat)
Ngomhla wenjabula,
sizohamba naye. (Repeat)

We will walk with God, my brothers,
we will walk with God.
We will walk with God, my sisters,
we will walk with God.
We will go rejoicing, till the kingdom has come. *(Repeat)*

Here is a magnificent recessional from Swaziland which can be easily taught in two or four parts. A phonetic version of the African text is:
   Seezohamba naayay.
   Goomshla wenjaboola

This song is featured on the album ONE IS THE BODY.

Now that evening falls

Tune: 'TAKING LEAVE', John L. Bell.

1. Now that evening falls,
gently fades the light;
moon replaces sun
and day takes leave of night.

2. Gratitude we raise
for the day that's done
and for what, tomorrow,
waits to be begun.

3. Gladly we commit
to God's gracious care
those we love and long for,
those whose lives we share.

4. Glory be to God,
glory to God's son,
glory to the Spirit
ever three in one.

This is a simple vesper hymn for the ending of the day, best sung in harmony by a quartet or choir with the whole assembly singing the final verse in unison.

Now that day is done

Tune: 'TARENMOT', John L. Bell.

1. *Cantor:*   Now that day is done,
    ALL: NOW THAT DAY IS DONE,
    Cantor: Jesus is with us;
    ALL: JESUS IS WITH US, NOW THAT DAY IS DONE.

2. Through the darkest night ...
3. In each hurt and hope ...
4. Breath within our breath ...

5. Making all things new ...
6. Till we meet again ...
7. Now that day is done ...

Here is a simple two-part vesper which is easily taught and remembered. Other verses may be added or substituted ad lib.

Journey prayers

Tune: 'QUAZELTANANGO', John L. Bell.

Moderato ♩ = ca. 60-63

Dm7 — G7

GOD'S GOS - PEL OF LIFE SHALL KEEP YOU;

Cmaj7 — F

GOD'S GOS - PEL SHALL SHEL - TER YOU FROM

B♭maj7 — E7/B — A — A7

HARM, MA - LICE AND E - VIL, AND FROM ALL DIS - TRESS.

Dm7 — G7

CHRIST SHALL HIM - SELF SHEP - HERD YOU, EN -

Cmaj7 — F

FOLD - ING YOU ON EVE - RY SIDE; WHERE -

B♭maj7 — E7/B — A

E - VER YOU MAY TRA - VEL HE'LL BE WITH YOU.

1. Bless to me, O God, the earth un-der my foot; bless the path on which I wan - der. Bless to me, O God, the things that I de - sire; bless to me, O God, my rest.

GOD'S GOSPEL OF LIFE SHALL KEEP YOU;
GOD'S GOSPEL SHALL SHELTER YOU
    FROM HARM, MALICE AND EVIL,
AND FROM ALL DISTRESS.
CHRIST SHALL HIMSELF SHEPHERD YOU,
ENFOLDING YOU ON EVERY SIDE;
WHEREVER YOU MAY TRAVEL HE'LL BE WITH YOU.

1. Bless to me, O God, the earth under my foot;
    bless the path on which I wander.
    Bless to me, O God, the things that I desire;
    bless to me, O God, my rest.

2. Bless to me, O God, the thoughts filling my mind;
    bless my yearning and my loving.
    Bless to me, O God, the hope deep in my heart;
    bless my seeing and my eyes.

The text for this song is derived from two ancient Celtic poems collected in the Western Isles at the end of the 19th century by the Gaelic scholar Alexander Carmichael. The song is particularly appropriate for a service of leave-taking or the commissioning of someone about to work overseas.

A choral version of this and another ancient Celtic song is available form the GIA Catalogue, G–5169, and both are featured on the album TAKE THIS MOMENT.

Your will be done

Tune: 'YOUR WILL BE DONE', John L. Bell.

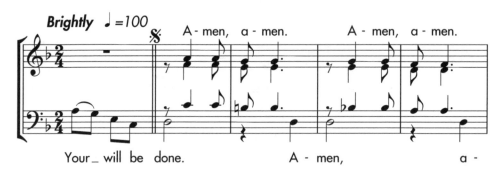

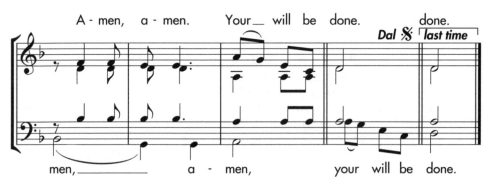

Paraphrase (from the Lord's Prayer) & music by John L. Bell, copyright © 2002 WGRG, Iona Community, Glasgow, Scotland.

Amen, amen.
Amen, amen.
Amen, amen.
Your will be done.

Recessionals are best when they can be sung without music, and when the congregation is singing in harmony. This is the intention of the above piece.
Teach the parts in this sequence – soprano, alto, tenor, bass – and when singing bring them in in the same order. Though the bass effectively begins the song, it is best to keep that part as the last entry, unless the choir or congregation know it well.

Now go in peace

Tune: 'JUNKANOO', Caribbean traditional.

Now go in peace, now go in love, from the Fa-ther a-bove. Je - sus Christ the Son stay with you till the day is done. Ho-ly Spi-rit en - cir-cle you in all you think and do. Once a - gain, God's bless-ing be with us. A - men. Now go in

Now go in peace, now go in love,
from the Father above.
Jesus Christ the Son stay with you
till the day is done.
Holy Spirit encircle you
in all you think and do.
Once again God's blessing be with us.
Amen.

This round was derived from a Scotsman who got it from second-generation Caribbeans living in Coventry. It encourages believers to exercise their priestly prerogative of blessing each other in the name of the Lord. It is best to sing the song in unison two or three times before breaking into the four-part round.

Alphabetical Index of First Lines and Titles

(Where different, titles are shown in italics)

The Iona Community

The Iona Community, founded in 1938 by the Revd George MacLeod, then a parish minister in Glasgow, is an ecumenical Christian community committed to seeking new ways of living the Gospel in today's world. Initially working to restore part of the medieval abbey on Iona, the Community today remains committed to 'rebuilding the common life' through working for social and political change, striving for the renewal of the church with an ecumenical emphasis, and exploring new, more inclusive approaches to worship, all based on an integrated understanding of spirituality.

The Community now has over 240 Members, about 1500 Associate Members and around 1500 Friends. The Members – women and men from many denominations and backgrounds (lay and ordained), living throughout Britain with a few overseas – are committed to a fivefold Rule of devotional discipline, sharing and accounting for use of time and money, regular meeting, and action for justice and peace.

At the Community's three residential centres – the Abbey and the MacLeod Centre on Iona, and Camas Adventure Camp on the Ross of Mull – guests are welcomed from March to October and over Christmas. Hospitality is provided for over 110 people, along with a unique opportunity, usually through week-long programmes, to extend horizons and forge relationships through sharing an experience of the common life in worship, work, discussion and relaxation. The Community's shop on Iona, just outside the Abbey grounds, carries an attractive range of books and craft goods.

The Community's administrative headquarters are in Glasgow, which also serves as a base for its work with young people, the Wild Goose Resource Group working in the field of worship, a bi-monthly magazine, *Coracle*, and a publishing house, Wild Goose Publications.

For information on the Iona Community contact:
The Iona Community
Fourth Floor, Savoy House,
140 Sauchiehall Street, Glasgow G2 3DH, UK
Phone: 0141 332 6343   e-mail: ionacomm@gla.iona.org.uk   web: www.iona.org.uk

For enquiries about visiting Iona, please contact:
Iona Abbey, Isle of Iona, Argyll PA76 6SN, UK
Phone: 01681 700404   e-mail: ionacomm@iona.org.uk

The Wild Goose Resource and Worship Groups

The Wild Goose Resource Group is an expression of the Iona Community's commitment to the renewal of public worship. Based in Glasgow, the Group has four members (Alison Adam, John Bell, Graham Maule and Mairi Munro) who are employed full-time and who lead workshops and seminars throughout Britain and abroad.

From 1984 to 2001, the four WGRG workers were also part of the Wild Goose Worship Group. The WGWG consisted of around sixteen, predominantly lay, people at any one time, who came from a variety of occupational and denominational backgrounds. Over the 17 years of its existence, it was the WGWG who tested, as well as promoted, the material in this book.

The task of both groups has been to develop and identify new methods and materials to enable the revitalisation of congregational song, prayer and liturgy. The songs and liturgical material have now been translated and used in many countries across the world as well as being frequently broadcast on radio and television.

The WGRG publishes a twice-yearly newsletter, GOOSEgander, to enable friends and supporters to keep abreast of WGRG developments. If you would like to find out about subscribing to GOOSEgander, please contact:

The Wild Goose Resource Group
Iona Community
Fourth Floor, Savoy House
140 Sauchiehall Street
Glasgow G2 3DH, Scotland.
Tel: 0141 332 6343   Fax: 0141 332 1090
e-mail: wgrg@gla.iona.org.uk
web: www.iona.org.uk/wgrg.html

Wild Goose Publications, the publishing house of the Iona Community established in the Celtic Christian tradition of St Columba, produces books, tapes and CDs on:

- holistic spirituality
- social justice
- political and peace issues
- healing
- innovative approaches to worship
- song in worship, including the work of the Wild Goose Resource Group
- material for meditation and reflection

If you would like to find out more about our books, tapes and CDs, please contact us at:

Wild Goose Publications
Fourth Floor, Savoy House
140 Sauchiehall Street,
Glasgow G2 3DH, UK

Tel. +44 (0)141 332 6292
Fax +44 (0)141 332 1090
e-mail: admin@ionabooks.com

or visit our website at
www.ionabooks.com
for details of all our products and online sales